T0113611

BREAKING
GENERATIONAL
CURSES

"EVERY GENERATION HAS A CURSE, BUT
EVERY CURSE CAN BE BROKEN"
~BE THE BREAKER~

CHRISTINA NANCE

authorHOUSE®

AuthorHouse™
1663 Liberty Drive
Bloomington, IN 47403
www.authorhouse.com
Phone: 833-262-8899

Published by AuthorHouse 02/11/2022

ISBN: 978-1-6655-5197-7 (sc)
ISBN: 978-1-6655-5196-0 (e)

Print information available on the last page.

Scripture are from the Holy Bible, King James Version (Authorized Version). First published in 1611. Quoted from the KJV Classic Reference Bible, Copyright © 1983 by The Zondervan Corporation.

This book is printed on acid-free paper.

Breaking generational curses....

To heal from a generational curse, you must acknowledge it.

Sometimes if you write things out, it's easier for you to accept it. Many times, we tuck things away, because if we don't speak on it, it never happened.

This book/journal will help you remember who you once were, who you currently are, and who you will become.

~Ezekiel 18:20~

The soul that sinneth, it shall die. The son shall not bear the iniquity of the father, neither shall the father bear the iniquity of the son: the righteousness of the righteous shall be upon him and the wickedness of the wicked shall be upon him.

What are Generational Curses?

The effect on a person of things that their ancestors did, believed or practiced in the past. A consequence of an ancestor's actions, beliefs and sins passed down.

The different types of Generational Curses:

*Poverty

*Family Stability

*Mental Illness

*Sinful Patterns

*Divorce

*Hereditary

*Molestation

*Verbal/Physical Abuse

*Masturbation

*Emotional Neglect

*Resentment

Generational Curses can be broken IF...

*You are willing to acknowledge them

*You are willing to forgive

*You can sit down and openly speak with everyone affected

*You are open to figuring the root of the curse out

As we move forward in your journal, we will go through a few Generational Curses. If you weren't affected by a curse, you are one of the lucky ones...not everyone was lucky as you.

Some of the curses may take days to get through, and that is okay. This is your journal, your feelings, and your healing time. Some curses may trigger memories you had tucked away, now is the time to release them.

Allow them tears to flow freely and begin your healing process!!

"You are not your situation…you are a SURVIVOR"

~C. Nance~

POVERTY

~THE STATE OF BEING POOR~

"Anyone who has struggled with POVERTY knows
how extremely expensive it is to be poor"

~JAMES BALDWIN~

*Did you grow up in POVERTY?

*How did POVERTY affect you mentally?

_____

_____

_____

_____

_____

_____

_____

_____

_____

_____

_____

_____

_____

_____

_____

_____

_____

_____

_____

_____

_____

_____

_____

*Did POVERTY give you a negative aspect on life?

_____

_____

_____

_____

_____

_____

_____

_____

_____

_____

_____

_____

_____

_____

_____

_____

_____

_____

_____

_____

_____

_____

_____

*What have you done to change your aspect on POVERTY?

_____

_____

_____

_____

_____

_____

_____

_____

_____

_____

_____

_____

_____

_____

_____

_____

_____

_____

_____

_____

_____

_____

_____

_____

*What can you do to help change POVERTY in your community?

_____
_____
_____
_____
_____
_____
_____
_____
_____
_____
_____
_____
_____
_____
_____
_____
_____
_____
_____
_____
_____
_____
_____
_____
_____

FAMILY STABILITY

~THE CONSISTENCY OF FAMILY ACTIVITIES AND ROUTINES~

'So much of what is best in us is bound up in our love of family, that it remains the measure of our stability because it measures our sense of loyalty~

~HANIEL LONG~

*Do you feel you came from a stable family?

_____

_____

_____

_____

_____

_____

_____

_____

_____

_____

_____

_____

_____

_____

_____

_____

_____

_____

_____

_____

_____

_____

*Did you grow up in a household with both parents? If not, what was your family dynamic?

_____

_____

_____

_____

_____

_____

_____

_____

_____

_____

_____

_____

_____

_____

_____

_____

_____

_____

_____

_____

_____

_____

_____

_____

*Did your family have daily routines such as, chores, sit down dinners, talks, homework time, etc?

_____

_____

_____

_____

_____

_____

_____

_____

_____

_____

_____

_____

_____

_____

_____

_____

_____

_____

_____

_____

_____

_____

_____

_____

_____

*Did your family discuss values, goals, and morals of life?

_____

_____

_____

_____

_____

_____

_____

_____

_____

_____

_____

_____

_____

_____

_____

_____

_____

_____

_____

_____

_____

_____

*Do you practice the same structure with your family today? Why or why not?

_____

_____

_____

_____

_____

_____

_____

_____

_____

_____

_____

_____

_____

_____

_____

_____

_____

_____

_____

_____

_____

_____

Mental Breaktime

When was the last time you LAUGHED? Like tears and snot running down your face, bent over holding your stomach LAUGH!! Write about that time for a moment:

PHYSICAL ABUSE

~ANY INTENTIONAL ACT CAUSING INJURY OR TRAUMA TO ANOTHER PERSON OR ANIMAL BY WAY OF BODILY CONTACT~

"Nobody abuses us more than we abuse ourselves"

~DON MIGUEL RUIZ~

*Were you raised in a household where you witnessed Physical Abuse?

_____

_____

_____

_____

_____

_____

_____

_____

_____

_____

_____

_____

_____

_____

_____

_____

_____

_____

_____

_____

_____

_____

*How did witnessing the abuse affect you?

_____

_____

_____

_____

_____

_____

_____

_____

_____

_____

_____

_____

_____

_____

_____

_____

_____

_____

_____

_____

_____

_____

_____

*Did you grow up being an abuser or being abused?

_____

_____

_____

_____

_____

_____

_____

_____

_____

_____

_____

_____

_____

_____

_____

_____

_____

_____

_____

_____

_____

_____

_____

*Do you feel you turned out that way because of the Physical Abuse you witnessed?

_____

_____

_____

_____

_____

_____

_____

_____

_____

_____

_____

_____

_____

_____

_____

_____

_____

_____

_____

_____

_____

_____

_____

*Have you ever been in an abusive relationship? If so, did you stay or go?

_____

_____

_____

_____

_____

_____

_____

_____

_____

_____

_____

_____

_____

_____

_____

_____

_____

_____

_____

_____

_____

_____

_____

*If you did stay, was it because you witnessed your parents stay and fight through it?

_____

_____

_____

_____

_____

_____

_____

_____

_____

_____

_____

_____

_____

_____

_____

_____

_____

_____

_____

_____

_____

_____

*At what point did you say enough is enough? If you are still in an abusive relationship, what is stopping you from leaving?

_____

_____

_____

_____

_____

_____

_____

_____

_____

_____

_____

_____

_____

_____

_____

_____

_____

_____

_____

_____

_____

_____

_____

_____

*If you have children, how do you think it will affect them seeing their parents in an abusive relationship?

_____
_____
_____
_____
_____
_____
_____
_____
_____
_____
_____
_____
_____
_____
_____
_____
_____
_____
_____
_____
_____
_____
_____
_____

*Once you find the strength to fight your abuser back, they will start to abuse another person in your house. Who would that person be...?

_____

_____

_____

_____

_____

_____

_____

_____

_____

_____

_____

_____

_____

_____

_____

_____

_____

_____

_____

_____

_____

_____

_____

*How will that make you feel? Will that be the last straw?

_____

_____

_____

_____

_____

_____

_____

_____

_____

_____

_____

_____

_____

_____

_____

_____

_____

_____

_____

_____

_____

_____

Why is it that we make excuses for our abusers…?

*Oh, they had a bad day at work
*Oh, they had too many drinks
*Oh, that's just how they are
*Oh, they were abused and know no other way

At what point do we stop making excuses for them?

You and only YOU, know when enough is enough!!

Anyone condoning someone being Physically Abused
in front of them is just as guilty as the abuser...

Mental Breaktime

If you had a chance to go back and have a conversation with your younger self, what age would you choose? What advice would you give yourself?

SINFUL PATTERNS

~TAINTED WITH, MARKED BY, OR FULL OF SIN...SUCH AS TO MAKE ONE FEEL GUILTY~

"When you are guilty, it is not your sins you hate, but yourself..."

~ANTHONY DE MELLO~

*What sinful patterns do you deal with daily?

_____

_____

_____

_____

_____

_____

_____

_____

_____

_____

_____

_____

_____

_____

_____

_____

_____

_____

_____

_____

_____

_____

_____

*How have these patterns affected you?

_____

_____

_____

_____

_____

_____

_____

_____

_____

_____

_____

_____

_____

_____

_____

_____

_____

_____

_____

_____

_____

_____

_____

_____

*What steps have you taken to break these sinful patterns?

_____

_____

_____

_____

_____

_____

_____

_____

_____

_____

_____

_____

_____

_____

_____

_____

_____

_____

_____

_____

_____

_____

_____

_____

_____

_____

_____

_____

_____

"Sinful and forbidden pleasures are like poisoned bread; they may satisfy appetite for the moment, but there is death in them at the end."

-Tyrone Edwards-

ADDICTION

~THE FACT OR CONDITION OF BEING ADDICTED TO A PARTICULAR SUBSTANCE, THING OR ACTIVITY~

"People become attached to their burdens sometimes more than the burdens are attached to them"

~GEORGE BERNARD SHAW~

*What type of addiction(s) did your family struggle with?

_____

_____

_____

_____

_____

_____

_____

_____

_____

_____

_____

_____

_____

_____

_____

_____

_____

_____

_____

_____

_____

_____

*How did the addiction(s) affect your family?

_____

_____

_____

_____

_____

_____

_____

_____

_____

_____

_____

_____

_____

_____

_____

_____

_____

_____

_____

_____

_____

_____

_____

_____

*Is your family still suffering from those addiction(s)?

_____
_____
_____
_____
_____
_____
_____
_____
_____
_____
_____
_____
_____
_____
_____
_____
_____
_____
_____
_____
_____
_____
_____
_____

*How did those addiction(s) affect you?

_____

_____

_____

_____

_____

_____

_____

_____

_____

_____

_____

_____

_____

_____

_____

_____

_____

_____

_____

_____

_____

_____

_____

_____

_____

*Are you currently dealing with an addiction(s)?

_____

_____

_____

_____

_____

_____

_____

_____

_____

_____

_____

_____

_____

_____

_____

_____

_____

_____

_____

_____

_____

_____

_____

_____

*Have you reached out for help with your addiction(s)?

_____

_____

_____

_____

_____

_____

_____

_____

_____

_____

_____

_____

_____

_____

_____

_____

_____

_____

_____

_____

_____

_____

_____

_____

*What steps have you taken to prevent these addiction(s) moving to the next generation?

_____

_____

_____

_____

_____

_____

_____

_____

_____

_____

_____

_____

_____

_____

_____

_____

_____

_____

_____

_____

_____

_____

_____

Mental Breaktime

Take this time to take an inventory of your life. Remove individuals who is not adding to your life.

MOLESTATION

~SEXUAL ASSAULT OR ABUSE
OF A PERSON, ESPECIALLY A
WOMAN OR CHILD...THE ACTION
OF PESTERING OR HARASSING
SOMEONE IN AN AGGRESSIVE
OR PERSISTENT MANNER~

"There are wounds that never show on the body that are
deeper and more hurtful than anything that bleeds"

~LAURELL K HAMILTON~

45

If I had to choose a generational curse to focus on the most, this would be it. Molestation is something most families tend to hide within their families. Try to make excuses for the actions of the family member doing the molesting.

They'll say things such as "oh he not right in the head" or "they didn't know what they were doing" or "they're acting out because it happened to them".

*Were you ever molested? If so, by who?

_____

_____

_____

_____

_____

_____

_____

_____

_____

_____

_____

_____

_____

_____

_____

_____

_____

_____

_____

_____

_____

_____

_____

*Did you ever tell someone you were molested? What was their response?

_____

_____

_____

_____

_____

_____

_____

_____

_____

_____

_____

_____

_____

_____

_____

_____

_____

_____

_____

_____

_____

_____

_____

_____

_____

*Were you forced to be around your molester?

_____

_____

_____

_____

_____

_____

_____

_____

_____

_____

_____

_____

_____

_____

_____

_____

_____

_____

_____

_____

_____

_____

*Do you still see your molester at family gatherings?

_____

_____

_____

_____

_____

_____

_____

_____

_____

_____

_____

_____

_____

_____

_____

_____

_____

_____

_____

_____

_____

_____

_____

_____

*How did it affect you mentally?

*How did it affect you emotionally?

_____

_____

_____

_____

_____

_____

_____

_____

_____

_____

_____

_____

_____

_____

_____

_____

_____

_____

_____

_____

_____

_____

_____

_____

_____

*Have you ever witnessed someone being molested before? Did you stop them?

_____

_____

_____

_____

_____

_____

_____

_____

_____

_____

_____

_____

_____

_____

_____

_____

_____

_____

_____

_____

_____

_____

_____

*Were you threatened by your molester?

_____

_____

_____

_____

_____

_____

_____

_____

_____

_____

_____

_____

_____

_____

_____

_____

_____

_____

_____

_____

_____

_____

_____

_____

_____

_____

*If you were molested, did you find yourself being overprotected with your children?

_____
_____
_____
_____
_____
_____
_____
_____
_____
_____
_____
_____
_____
_____
_____
_____
_____
_____
_____
_____
_____
_____
_____
_____
_____
_____
_____

Majority of people won't understand the mindset of someone that was MOLESTED.

They don't realize you were:

*Forced to grow up
*Questioned your sexuality
*Suffered from low self-esteem
*As you get older, its hard to do or accept certain things in relationships
*Certain things are triggers and can cause panic attacks

*Did your family make you feel like you were the one in the wrong?

_____

_____

_____

_____

_____

_____

_____

_____

_____

_____

_____

_____

_____

_____

_____

_____

_____

_____

_____

_____

_____

_____

*Did you press charges against your molester? Why or why not?

_____

_____

_____

_____

_____

_____

_____

_____

_____

_____

_____

_____

_____

_____

_____

_____

_____

_____

_____

_____

_____

_____

_____

Sometimes it is hard to face your molester, because your molester is normally a loved one. A loved one who should have protected you. A loved one who you felt should know right from wrong. A loved one who others witnessed do the same thing and remained quiet.

Take a moment and write your molester a letter. Be open and let them know how they affected you mentally and emotionally. Let them know you're not that scared little child no more.

This will allow you to begin your healing process.

Mental Breaktime

Take this time to write a letter to someone who caused you pain, someone who caused your hurt.

I call these "uninterrupted conversations". These conversations are therapeutic and help you begin your healing. You can either mail the letters to the individuals or burn it after you write it.

RESENTMENT

~BITTER INDIGNATION AT HAVING BEEN TREATED UNFAIRLY~

"Resentment is like drinking poison and then hoping it will kill your enemies"

~NELSON MANDELA~

There are different types of resentments:

*Anger
*Uneasiness
*Frustration
*Hard Feelings
*Hostility
*Manipulation

*What or who is the root of your resentment?

_____

_____

_____

_____

_____

_____

_____

_____

_____

_____

_____

_____

_____

_____

_____

_____

_____

_____

_____

_____

_____

_____

_____

_____

_____

*What type of resentment do you feel you experience?

_____

_____

_____

_____

_____

_____

_____

_____

_____

_____

_____

_____

_____

_____

_____

_____

_____

_____

_____

_____

_____

_____

_____

*How has the resentment affected you mentally and emotionally?

_____

_____

_____

_____

_____

_____

_____

_____

_____

_____

_____

_____

_____

_____

_____

_____

_____

_____

_____

_____

_____

_____

_____

*What steps are you taking to heal from the resentment?

_____

_____

_____

_____

_____

_____

_____

_____

_____

_____

_____

_____

_____

_____

_____

_____

_____

_____

_____

_____

_____

_____

_____

Forgiveness begins with YOU!!

Forgiving someone, doesn't mean you agree with their actions.

Forgiving someone doesn't mean you will
forget what they did to you.

In order to heal, you must forgive those
that caused your hurt and pain.

My testimony to MY mother:

Over the years we've struggled and this past year we've gotten closer. There was a lot of resentment and a lot of deep-rooted pain and uninterrupted conversations that was needed. There was a lot of hidden childhood trauma that wasn't shared until decades later and necessary tears that needed to be shed.

Sometimes as the oldest child, you are left feeling unwanted, unloved, like a burden and useless. As the oldest child, you experience ALL the trails and tribulations and struggles, heart aches, and disappointments your mother go through.

Growing up as the oldest child, it was hard for ME to see my mother happy with her other children, because she didn't have that same happiness with me. (She had me you, so we grew together)

It was hard being a kid, because I had to step up and be there while my mom worked a fulltime job in the day as a Dental Assistant and went to school fulltime at night to become a Nurse.

We weren't the type of family to express ourselves, such as saying "I Love You" (a curse finally broken) we felt we showed it by our actions.

It's never too late to start the healing process on broken bonds! It's never too late to acknowledge YOUR wrong in situations and set boundaries! It's never too late start over in a mother/ daughter bond or any bond!

My mom is not perfect, but neither am I!

I've never shared with my mom how proud I am of her! I've never told my mom that on the days she felt like giving up, I was praying for her to keep going! I love you mom and I am so PROUD of you!!!

#breakinggenerationalcureses

I hope this journal helped you to begin your healing process. I know it is hard to seek therapy or outside help. I also know that keeping things in is not healthy and will one day break you down.

This is your personal therapy, behind closed doors. There may be a time that you will need to see a therapist and there is nothing wrong with that. Sometimes it takes an outsider to help you.

Seeking therapy does not make you a weak individual!!

Remember, there is no time limit on the healing process. Healing is just like grieving. There are five different stages, and everyone will go through each stage at different times in life.

Five Stages of Grief and Healing:

*Denial and Isolation

*Anger

*Bargaining

*Depression

*Acceptance

Printed in the United States
by Baker & Taylor Publisher Services